Abiogenesis and Life from Dirt: The Andrew Crosse Experiment

Andrew Crosse and William H. Weekes

Copyright © 2015
All rights reserved.
Published by The Book Shed
978-1-943392-00-1

CONTENTS

Introduction   1

Crosse's Experiment   5

Recreation of Crosse's Experiment   25

INTRODUCTION

In the year of 1837 Andrew Crosse endeavored to create synthetic crystal formations with silicates, water, and electricity. A couple weeks into the experiment, Crosse saw tiny crystal nucleations. Success, he thought. But, in the weeks to come he would notice something revolutionary. These crystal formations were developing the exact anatomy of an insect from the genus *acarus*! Eventually, these insect mineralizations dislodged from their rocky birthplace and began moving around. They even responded to external stimulus, such as light, implying that they developed some sort of sensory ability.

When Crosse shared his results with the local community, an outrage ensued. "Only God can create" yelled the angry community. Ironically, Crosse had given the best evidence for life being created from dirt, beyond biological means. Abiogenesis. Even more ironic, the initial conditions in Genesis include earth, water, and electricity:

1. The earth (Genesis 1:1) is comprised of about 70% silicates in its crust.

2. Water (Genesis 1:2).

3. Electricity is implied when light becomes present (Genesis 1:3), because light is electromagnetic radiation. Electricity is a form of electromagnetic radiation.

Crosse demonstrated that life can arise from ways we have yet to understand through modern science. Many laugh and say his experiment was simply infested with the ova of the described insect. Crosse discusses his various methods of aseptic technique which insist that this was not the case. Even more convincing, his experiment was successfully recreated by William H Weekes of the London Electrical Society. Both Crosse's and Weekes' full experiment are contained within this book. Weekes' recreation describes roasting the equipment at over 400 degrees, which without a doubt would denature any sort of biological egg not meant to withstand such temperatures.

Regardless of any implications regarding the creation of life, this is a truly amazing experiment that deserves to be known by every person seeking answers to life's grandest questions. Many will wonder why more people don't know about this. My best guess is because it is inexplicable. No means of science could begin to explain how this abiogenesis occurs. It is as if life is encoded in electricity, or rather, light.

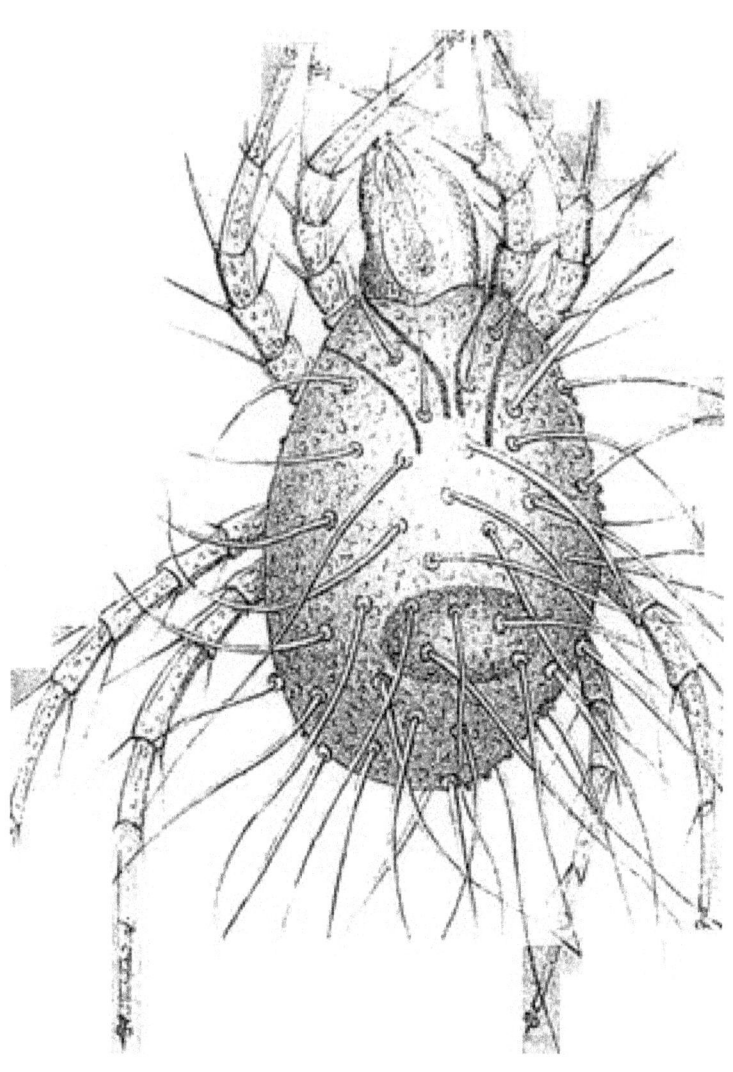

4

II. Description of some Experiments made with the Voltaic Battery, by Andrew Crosse, Esq of Broomfield, near Taunton, for the purpose of producing Crystals; in the process of which Experiments certain Insects constantly appeared. Communicated in a Letter dated 27th December, 1837, addressed to the Secretary of the London Electrical Society.

Read 20th January, 1838.
(Figures are at the end)

My dear Sir,

I trust that the gentlemen who compose the "Electrical Society" will not imagine that because I have so long delayed answering their request, to furnish the Society through you. as its organ, with a full account of my electrical experiments, in which a certain insect made its unexpected appearance, that such delay has been occasioned by any desire of withholding what I have to state from the Society in particular, or the public at large. 1 am delighted to find that at last, late, though not the less called for, a body of scientific gentlemen have linked themselves together for the sake of exploring and making public those mysteries, which hitherto, under a variety of names, and ascribed to all causes but the true one, have eluded the grasp of men of research, and served to perplex, perhaps, rather than to afford sufficient data to theorise upon. It is true that much has been done in the course of a few years, and that which has been done only affords the strongest reason for believing that vastly more remains to be done. It would be presumptuous in me to enumerate the services of a Davy, a Faraday, and many other great men at home, or a Volta and an Ampere, with a host of others abroad. These distinguished men have laid the foundations, on which their successors ought to endeavour to erect a building worthy of the scale in which it has been commenced. Electricity is no longer the paltry confined science which it was once fancied to be, making its appearance only from the friction of glass or wax. employed in childish purposes, serving as a trick for the school boy, or a nostrum for the quack. But it is, even now, though in its infancy, proved to be most intimately connected with all operations in chemistry, with magnetism, with light and caloric; apparently a properly belonging to all matter, perhaps ranging through all space, from sun to sun, from planet to planet, and not improbably the secondary cause of every change in the animal, mineral, vegetable, and gaseous systems. It is to determine whether this be or not, the case, as far as human faculties can determine, to ascertain what rank in the tree of science electricity is to hold; to endeavour to find out to what useful purposes it might be applied, that I conceive is the object of your Society, and I shall at all times be ready and willing, as a member, to contribute my quota of information to its support, knowing well, that however little it might be, it will be as kindly received as it is humbly offered. It is most unpleasing to my feelings to glance at myself as an individual, but I have met with so much virulence and abuse, so much calumny and misrepresentation, in consequence of the experiments which I am about to detail, and which it seems in this nineteenth century a crime to have made, that I must state, not for the sake of myself (for I utterly scorn all such misrepresentations), but for the sake of truth and the science which I follow, that I am neither an "Atheist," nor a "Materialist," nor a "self-imagined creator," but a humble and lowly reverencer of that Great Being, whose laws my accusers scorn wholly to have lost sight of. More than this, it is my conviction, that science is only valuable as a mean to a greater end. I can assure you, sir, that I attach no particular value to any experiment that I have made, and that my feelings and habits are much more of a retiring than an obtruding character; and I care not if what I have done be entirely overthrown, if truth be elicited. The following is a plain and correct account of the experiments alluded to.

In the course of my endeavours to form artificial minerals by a long-continued electric action on fluids holding in solution such substances as were necessary to my purpose, I had recourse to every variety of contrivance which I could think of, so that, on the one hand, I might be enabled to keep up a never-failing electrical current of greater or less intensity, or quantity, or both, as the case seemed to require; and on the other hand, that the solutions made use of should be exposed to the electric action in the manner best calculated to effect the object in view. Amongst other contrivances, I constructed a wooden frame, of about two feet in height, consisting of four legs proceeding from a shelf at the bottom supporting another at the top, and containing a third in the middle. Each of these shelves was about seven inches square. The upper one was pierced with an aperture, in which was fixed a funnel of Wedgewood ware, within which rested a quart basin on a circular piece of mahogany placed within the funnel. When this basin was filled with a fluid, a strip of flannel wetted with the same, was suspended over the edge of the basin anil inside the funnel which, acting as a syphon, conveyed the fluid out of the basin, through the funnel, in successive drops. The middle shelf of the frame was likewise pierced with an aperture, in which was fixed a smaller funnel of glass, which supported a piece of somewhat porous red oxide of iron from Vesuvius, immediately under the dropping of the upper funnel. This stone was kept constantly electrified by means of two platina wires on either side of it, Connected with the poles of a Voltaic battery of nineteen pairs of five-inch line and copper single plates, in two porcelain troughs, the cells of which were filled at first with water and then of hydrochloric acid, but afterwards with water alone. I may here state, that in all my subsequent experiments relative to these insects, I filled the cells of the batteries employed with nothing but common water. The lower shelf merely supported a wide-mouthed bottle, to receive the drops as they fell front the second funnel. When the basin was nearly emptied, the fluid was poured back again from the bottle below into the basin above, without disturbing the position of the stone. It was by mere chance that I selected this volcanic substance, choosing it from its partial porosity ; nor do I believe that it had the slightest effect in the production of the insects to be described. The fluid with which I filled the basin was made as follows.

I reduced a piece of black flint to powder, having first exposed it to a red heat and quenched it in water to make it friable. Of this powder I took two ounces, and mixed them intensely with six ounces of carbonate of potassa. exposed them to a strong heat for fifteen minutes in a black lead crucible in an air furnace, and then poured the fused compound on an iron plate, reduced it to powder while still warm, poured boiling water on it, and kept it boiling for some minutes in a sand hath. The greater part of the soluble glass thus fused, was taken up by the water, together with a portion of alumina from the crucible. I should have used one of silver, but had none sufficiently large. To a portion of the silicate of potassa thus fitted, I added some boiling water to dilute it, and then slowly raided hydrochloric acid to supersaturation. A strange remark was made on this part of the experiment at the meeting of the British Association at Liverpool, it being then gravely stated, that it impossible to add an acid to a silicate of potassa without precipitating the silica! This, of course, must be the case, unless the solution be diluted with water. My object in subjecting this fluid to a long-continued electric action through the intervention of a porous stone, was to form, if possible, crystals of silica at one of the poles of the battery, but I failed in accomplishing this by those means. On the fourteenth* day from the commencement of the experiment, I observed, through a lens, a few small whitish excrescences or nipples projecting from about the middle of the electrified stone, and nearly under the dropping of the fluid above. On the eighteenth* day these projections enlarged, and seven or eight filaments, each of them longer than the excrescence from which it grew, made their appearance on each of the nipples On the twenty-second* day these appearances were more elevated and distinct, and on the twenty-sixth day each figure assumed the form of a perfect insect, standing erect on a few bristles which formed its tail. Till this period I had no notion that these appearances were any other than an incipient mineral formation; but it was not until the twenty-eighth day, when I plainly perceived these little creatures move their legs that I felt any surprise, and I must own that when this took place, I was not a little astonished. I endeavoured to detach with the point of a needle, one or two of them from its position on the stone, but they immediately died, and I was obliged to wait patiently for a few days longer, when they separated themselves from the stone, and moved about at pleasure, although they had been for some time after their birth apparently averse to motion. In the course of a few weeks about a hundred of them made their appearance on the stone. I observed that at first each of them fixed itself for a considerable time in one spot, appearing, as far as I could judge, to feed by suction; but when a ray of light, from the sun was directed upon it, it seemed disturbed, and removed itself to the shaded part of the stone. Out of about a hundred insects, not above five or six were born on the south side of the stone. I examined some of them with the microscope, and observed that the smaller ones appeared to have only six legs, but the larger ones eight. It would be superfluous to attempt a description of these little mites when so excellent a one has been transmitted from I Paris. It seems that they are of the genus Acarus, but of a species not hitherto observed. I have had three separate formations of similar insects at different times, from fresh portions of the same fluid, with the same apparatus. As I considered the result of this experiment rather extraordinary, I made some of my friends acquainted with it, amongst whom were some highly scientific gentlemen, and they plainly perceived the insect in various states. I likewise transmitted some of them to one of our most distinguished physiologists in London, and the opinion of this gentleman, as well as of other eminent persons to whom he showed them, coincided with that of the gentlemen of the Academie des Sciences, as to their genus and species. I have never ventured an opinion as to the cause of their birth, and for a very good reason — I was unable to form one. The most simple solution of the problem which occurred to me, was, that they arose from ova deposited by insects floating in the atmosphere, and that they might possibly be hatched by the electric action. Still I could not imagine that an ovum could shoot out filaments, and that those filaments would become bristles; and moreover, I could not detect, on the closest examination, any remains of a shell. Again, we have no right to assume that electric action is necessary to vitality, until such fact shall have been most distinctly proved. I next imagined, as others have done, that they might have originated from the water, and consequently made a close examination of several hundred vessels, filled with the same water as that which held in solution the silicate of potassa, in the same room, which vessels constituted the cells of a large Voltaic battery, used without acid. In none of these vessels could I perceive the trace of an insect of that description. I likewise closely examined the crevices and most dusty parts of the room with no better success. In the course of some months, indeed, these insects so increased, that when they were strong enough to leave their moistened birthplace, they issued out in different directions, I suppose, in quest of food ; but they generally huddled together under a card or piece of paper in their neighbourhood, as if to avoid light and disturbance. In the course of my experiments upon other matters, I tilled a glass basin with a concentrated solution of silicate of potassa without acid, in the middle of which I placed a piece of brick, used in this neighbourhood for domestic purposes, and consisting mostly of silica. Two wires of platina connected either cud of the brick with the poles of a Voltaic battery of sixty-three pairs of plates, each about two inches square. After many months' action, silica in a gelatinous state formed in some quantity round the bottom of the brick, and as the solution evaporated, I replaced it by fresh additions, so that the outside of the glass basin being constantly wet by repeated overflowings, was, of course, constantly electrified. On this outside, as well as on the edge of the fluid within, I one day perceived the well-known whitish excrescence with its projecting filaments. In the course of time they increased in number, and as they successively burst into life, the whole table on which the apparatus stood, at last was covered with similar insects, which hid themselves wherever they could find a shelter. Some of them were of different sizes, there being a considerable difference in this respect between (be larger and smaller; and they were plainly perceptible to the naked eye as they nimbly crawled from one spot to another. I closely examined the table with a lens, but could perceive no such excrescence as that which marks their incipient state, on any part of it. While these effects were taking place in my electrical room, similar formations were making their appearance in another room, distant from the former. I had here placed on a table, three Voltaic batteries unconnected with each other. The first consisted of twenty pairs of two-inch plates, between the poles of which I placed a glass cylinder filled with a concentrated solution of silicate of potassa, in which was suspended a piece of clay slate by two platina wires connected with either pole of the battery. A piece of paper was placed on the top of the cylinder to keep out the dust. Alter many months' action, gelatinous silica in various forms was electrically attracted to the slate, which it coated in rather a singular manner, unnecessary here to describe. In the course of time I observed similar insects in their incipient state forming around the edge of the fluid within the jar, which, when perfect, crawled about the inner surface of the paper with great activity. The second battery consisted of twenty pairs of cylinders, each equal to a four-inch plate. Between the poles of this I interposed a series of seven glass cylinders, filled with the following concentrated solutions: — 1. Nitrate of copper: 2. Sub-carbonate of potassa: 3. Sulphate of copper : 4. Green sulphate of iron : 5. Sulphate of zinc: 5. Water acidified with a minute portion of hydrochloric acid: Water poured on powdered metallic arsenic, resting on a copper cup, connected with the positive pole of the Battery. All these cylinders were electrically united together by arcs of sheet copper to that the same electric current passed through the whole of them.

After many months' action. and consequent formation of certain crystalline matters, which it is not my object here to notice, I observed similar excrescences with those before described at the edge of the fluid in every one of the cylinders, excepting the two which contained the carbonate of potassa, and the metallic arsenic; and in due time a host of insects made their appearance. It was curious to observe the crystallised nitrate and sulphate of copper, which formed by slow evaporation at the edge of the respective solutions, dotted here and there with these hairy excrescences. At the foot of each of the cylinders I had placed a paper ticket upon the table, and on lifting them up I found a little colony of insects under each, but no appearance whatever of their having been born under their respective papers, or on any part of the table. The third battery consisted of twenty pairs of cylinders, each equal to a three-inch plate. Between the poles of this I interposed likewise a series of six glass cylinders, filled with various solutions, in only one of which I obtained the insect. This contained a concentrated solution of silicate of potassa. A bent iron wire, one- fifth of an inch in diameter, in the form of an inverted syphon, was plunged some inches into this solution, and connected it with the positive pole, whilst a small coil of fine silver wire joined it with the negative.

After some months' electrical action, gelatinous silica enveloped both wires, but in much greater quantity at the positive pole; and in about eight months from the commencement of the experiment, on examining these two wires very minutely, by means of a lens, having removed them from the solution for that purpose, I plainly perceived one of these incipient insects upon the gelatinous silica on the silver wire, and about half an inch below the surface of the fluid, when replaced its original position. In the course of time, more insects made their appearance, till, at last, I counted at once three on the negative and twelve on the positive wire. Some of them were formed on the naked part of the wires, that is, on that port which was partially bare of gelatinous silica: but they were mostly imbedded more or less in the silica, with eight or ten filaments projecting from each beyond the silica. It was perfectly impossible to mistake them, after having made oneself master of their different appearances; and an occasional motion in the filaments of those that had been the longest formed was very perceptible, and observed by many of my visitors, without my having previously noticed the fact to them. Most of these productions took place from half to three-quarters of an inch under the surface of the fluid, which, as it evaporated very slowly. I kept to the same level by adding fresh portions. As some of these insects were formed on the inverted part of the syphon-shaped wire, I cannot imagine how they contrived to arrive at the surface, and to extricate themselves from the fluid; yet this they did repeatedly; their old places were vacated, and others were born in new ones. Whether they were in an imperfect state (except just at the commencement of their formation), or in a perfect one, they had all the distinguishing characteristic of bristles projecting from their bodies, which occasioned the French sarans to remark that they resembled a microscopic porcupine. I must not omit to state, that the room in which these three batteries were acting was kept almost constantly darkened. It was not my intention to make known these observations until I myself should be better informed about the matter. Chance led to the publication of an erroneous account of them, which I was under the necessity of explaining. It is so difficult to arrive at the truth, that mankind would do better to lend their assistance to explore what may be worth investigating, than to endeavour to crush in its bud that which might otherwise expand into a flower. In giving this account, I have merely stated those circumstances regarding the appearance of insects, which I have noticed during my investigations into the formation of mineral matters; existing in the stone or the silica; and have formed no visionary theory which I would travel out of my way to support. I have since repeated these latter experiments in a third room, in which there are now two batteries at work. One consisting of eleven pairs of cylinders, made of four-inch plates between the poles of which is placed a glass cylinder, filled with silicate of potassa, in which is suspended a piece of slate between two wires of platina, as before, and covered loosely with paper. Here, again, is another crop of insects formed. The other battery consists of twenty pairs of cylinders, the electric current of which is passed through six different solutions in glass cylinders, in three of which only is the insect formed, viz., 1st. in nitrate of copper; 2d. in sulphate of copper, in each of which the insect is only produced at the edge of the fluid, as far as I can make out; and 3d. by the old apparatus of coiled silver and iron wire in silicate of potassa, as before. There are now forming on the bottom of this positively electrified wire similar insects, at the distance of fully two inches below the surface of the fluid. On examining these, I have lately noticed a peculiar quality they possess whilst in an incipient state. After being kept some minutes out of the solution, they contract their filaments, so as, in some cases, wholly, and in others partially, to disappear. I at first thought they were destroyed; but, on examining the same spots, on the next day, they were as perceptible as before. In this respect, they seem not unlike the zoophytes, which adhere to the rocks on the seashore and which contract on the approach of a finger. I may likewise remark, that I have not been able to detect their eyes, even when viewed under a powerful microscope, although I once fancied I perceived them. The extreme heat of summer and cold of winter do not appear favourable to their production, which succeeds best, I think, in spring and autumn. As in the above account I have occasionally made use of the word "formation," I beg that it might be understood that I do not mean creation, or any thing approaching to it. I am not aware that I have any thing more to add, except the few remarks I shall conclude with.

1st I have not observed a formation of the insect, except on a moist and electrified surface, or under an electrified fluid. By this I do not mean to assert that electricity has any thing to do with their birth, as I have not made a sufficient number of experiments to prove or disprove it; and besides, I have not taken those necessary precautions which present themselves even to an unscientific view. These precautions are not so easy to observe as may at first sight appear. It is, however, my intention to repeat these experiments, by passing a stream of electricity through cylinders filled with various fluids under a glass receiver inverted over mercury, the greatest possible care being taken to shut out extraneous matter. Should there be those who blame me for not having done this before, to such I answer that, independent of a host of other hindrances, which it is not in my power to set aside, I have been closely pursuing a long train of experiments on the formation of crystalline matters by the electric agency, and now different modifications of the Voltaic battery; in which I am so interested, that none but the ardent can conceive what is not in my power to describe.

2dly. These insects do not appear to have originated from others similar to themselves, as they are formed in all cases with access of moisture, and in some cases two inches below the surface of the fluid in which they are born; and if a full grown and perfect insect be let fall into any fluid, it is infallibly drowned.

3dly. I believe they live for many weeks: occasionally I have found them dead in groups, apparently from want of food.

4thly. It has been frequently suggested to me to repeat these experiments without using the electric agency; but this would be by no means satisfactory, let the event be what it would. It is well known that saline matters are easily crystallized without subjecting them to the electric action ; but it by no means follows that, because artificial electricity is not applied, such crystals are formed without the electric influence. I have made so many experiments on electrical crystallization, that I am firmly convinced in my own mind, that electric attraction is the cause of the formation of every crystal, whether artificial electricity be applied or not. I am, however, well aware of the difficulty of getting at the truth in these matters, and of separating cause from effect. It has often occurred to me how it is that such numbers of animalcules are produced in flour and water, in pepper and water? also, the injects which infest fruit trees after a blight? Does not a chemical change take place in the water, and likewise in the sap of the tree previous to the appearance of these insects, and is or is not every chemical change produced by electric agency? In making these observations I seek to mislead no one. The book of nature is opened wide to our view by the Almighty power, and we must endeavour, as far as our feeble faculties will permit, to make a good use of it; always remembering, that however the timid may shrink from investigation, the more completely the Secrets of nature are laid bare, the more effectually will the power of that Great Being be manifested, who seems to have ordained, that

"Order is Heaven's first law."

I beg to remain, in the mean time, my dear Sir,
Your's, very sincerely,
ANDREW CROSSE

Broomfield,
December 27, 1837.

LONDON ELECTRICAL SOCIETY.

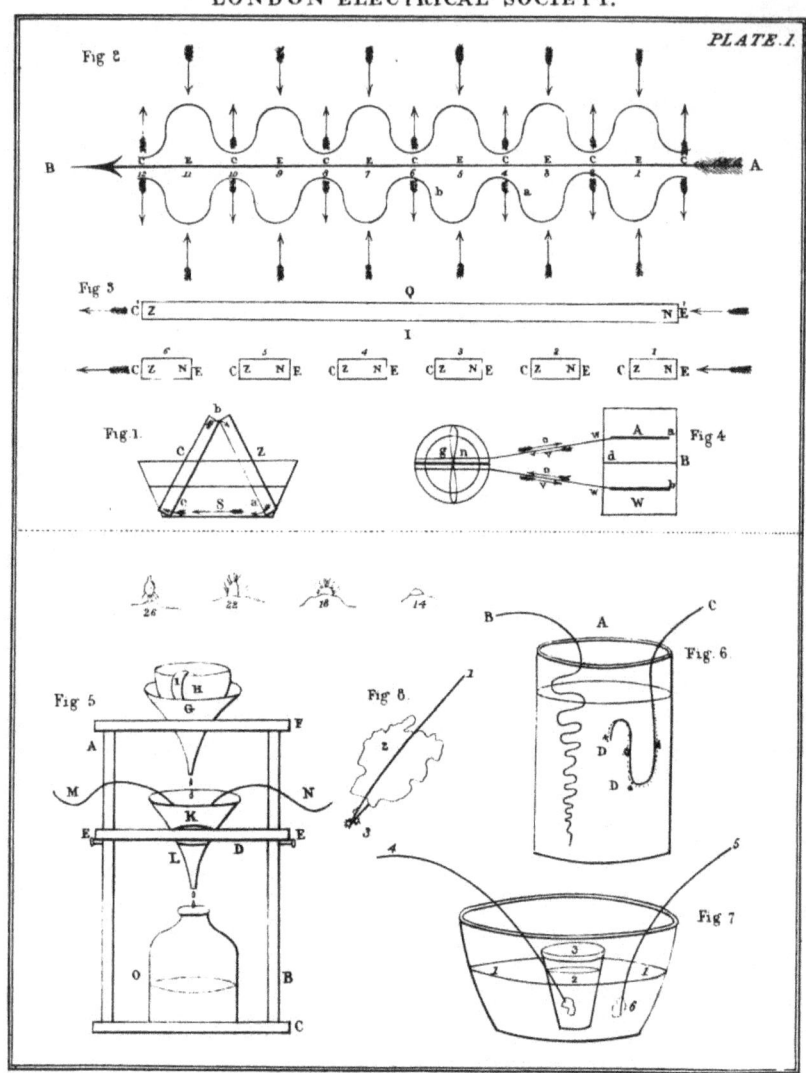

Tuesday, March 15.
Read: — Details of an experiment in which certain Insects, known as the Acarus Crossi, appeared incident to the long-continued operation of a Voltaic Current upon Silicate of Potass, within a close Atmosphere over Mercury. — By W. H. Weekes, Esq. Communicated by the Secretary.

The annals of philosophical research would probably fail to reveal a parallel to the amazing progress with which we cannot but recognize the advance of electrical science within the comparatively brief period of a few recent years. The universality of electric action incident to the development, not only of chemical phenomena, but also those dependent on mere physical change, is, I presume, too palpably evident to furnish henceforward the ingenuities of sophistry with materials for disputation, or permit even a temporary retreat for the most determined skepticism.

Upwards of half a century has now elapsed since the philosophic Franklin taught us the perfect identity of the lightning flash with an electric fluid artificially excited by human contrivance; and subsequent experimental researches have succeeded in familiarizing us with the important fact, that the energies of free electricity are seldom, if ever, found at entire rest in the atmosphere by which we are surrounded. Nor has the hand of science been content to trace the operations of this grand agent of nature in the air we breathe, or in the economy of a vast vegetable kingdom dispersed over every accessible and known portion of the earth's surface; but the spirit of inquiry has penetrated to the darksome recesses of the globe, and has at length divulged the secret spell by means of which form and order have been effectually maintained throughout the immense subterraneous mineral storehouse.

The most able physiologists have not hesitated to acknowledge an evident relation between electric action and some of the most remarkable phenomena of life, more especially as manifested through the medium of the nervous structure in the higher orders of animal being; and, certainly, their inferences have received very strong support, if not confirmation, from the direct employment of voltaic currents, during several recent postmortem and other experiments. That the same species of agency should have been resorted to as a secondary means of developing the principles of vitality to a class of animals vastly inferior as regards their apparent organization, seems a conclusion neither derogatory to the most exalted conceptions of a Creator, or presumptuous in those who delight to cultivate an acquaintance with the magnificent works of His hand.

I do not feel conscious that I have travelled out of my way merely for the sake of indulging in the few preceding remarks: they have been naturally suggested to me by unavoidable reflections on the ungenerous treatment not long since experienced in a very marked degree by one of the most disinterested lovers of truth and scientific inquiry whose labours have graced the annals of modem philosophy; and, I doubt not, it will at once be obvious to all who are conversant with the progress of British science, that my present allusions are directed to the celebrated voltaic experiments of Andrew Crosse, Esq.; one of the incidents of which, in the year 1837, was the appearance of a new species of insect, now denominated the Acarus Crossi, or Acarus galvanicus. I need scarcely remind the Society that the announcement of this singular fact, the birth, or development of acari in vast numbers, during the continuous operation of a voltaic current upon a porous Vesuvian iron-stone, kept constantly moistened by a saturated solution of silicate of potass, at the period in question, threw the learned world into a state of very unusual excitement.

Painful as it must ever be to the genuine lover of science to witness the diligence and research of its votaries assailed by calumny arid misrepresentation, I feel assured that no remarks of mine are needed to disengage the Broomfield experiments from the abuse of those who have sought to crush and misinterpret facts which, if carefully investigated, will ultimately conduct us to a more intimate acquaintance with the sublime laws of

Creative Wisdom. The experiments, however, which it is the object of this paper to detail, will, I trust, constitute a more powerful appeal to conviction than the most persuasive eloquence could command for the occasion. I shall, therefore, merely remind those who are interested in the inquiry, that a plain unvarnished report of Mr. Crosse's experiments, written by himself, will be found at page eleven of "The Transactions and the Proceedings of the London Electrical Society, from 1837 to 1840;" (included in this book) and at page one hundred and thirty-four of the same work, "A Translation of a Memoir Turpin at tire Academie des Sciences, Paris, On the Appearance of certain Insects in the Electrical Experiments of Mr. Crosse." The original memoir is illustrated by a drawing of the magnified insect, which drawing has been republished in this country, in an excellent lithographic plate, by W. Sturgeon, Esq., in the second volume of his Annals of Electricity, &c.

At a period not long subsequent to those experiments in which the Acarus Crossi first made its appearance, a train of agreeable circumstances, not necessary to be here particularized, procured me the favour of that gentleman's acquaintance ; and, during my visits to the hospitable mansion of Broomfield, I had the happiness to become familiar with the nature of his extraordinary researches, as well as his magnificent arrangements in regard to voltaic and atmospherical electricity. Finally, about the close of the year 1840, I undertook the course of an experimental investigation which constitutes the material of the present paper, subject to conditions which it was conceived would render nugatory all objections urged against the original experiments of Mr. Crosse.

I shall first endeavour minutely to describe the apparatus by means of which my experiments have been conducted, and then, following the example of my esteemed predecessor, submit a simple detail of every fact and circumstance which I think can be supposed to have the most remote bearing upon the eventual results.

In the apparatus a block of well-seasoned close-grained beech wood, an inch and a half in thickness, and ten inches square, which, after it had been slowly but thoroughly baked, received several successive coatings of linseed oil until saturation was obtained. Upon the upper plane of this block, and equidistant from its centre, it sunk to the depth of six-tenths of an inch, and four-tenths in width, a circular groove or channel, serving as a mercurial trough or valvular recess to the rim of the large bell glass seen in the sketch. The nature of this contrivance will, perhaps, be better illustrated by a sectional view of the block.
The air-bell is eight inches in height, four and a half inches in diameter at its base, and has a capacity of about one hundred and forty cubic inches. The neck of the bell is surmounted with a brass cap, which is provided with an orifice having the usual adaptation of a female screw, half an inch wide, for the reception of stop-cocks and other appendages usually employed in pneumatic chemistry.

A mercurial cup formed from a piece of glass tube half on inch in bore, and one and a half inches in length, the lower opening being closed with a good sound cork, is cemented to the outside of the bell glass, for the purpose of containing a small quantity of the metal; three-tenths of an inch beneath the surface of which dips the inferior aperture of the small bent glass tube while its other extremity has free communication with the inside of the air-bell, first passing through an excellent velvet cork occupying the opening of the brass cap already described.

Perpendicularly through the cork in the neck of the bell also descends a stout copper wire, m, nearly one-eighth of an inch diameter, and which is continued directly downwards, until it reaches to within some two inches of the glass vessel, n, and at about that distance it is firmly soldered to a wire of platina, one twenty-fifth of an inch in thickness, which being in the first instance bent from off the copper wire at a right angle thereto, subsequently makes a vertical descent to the bottom of the glass tumbler, n, where it terminates in a helix one-fourth of an inch in diameter.

The upper extremity of the copper wire, m, projects about two inches above the brass cap embracing the neck of the bell, and is there surmounted by the mercurial cup, o, formed in every respect similar to the one previously mentioned ; and through the cork bottom of this cup, to the extent of half an inch within the cavity thereof, the wire is made to penetrate, in order that perfect metallic contact may be established between it and one of the poles of a battery arrangement to be eventually employed.

I will here mention, that us soon as the bent tube and the wire m had been secured in their requisite positions, a quantity of hard red cement, composed of rosin, wax and Venetian red, in the usual proportions employed for mounting chemical apparatus, was melted and poured into the neck of the bell, so as completely to imbed the tube and wire to the depth of an inch at least, and thus effectually render the superior aperture impervious to air; the external surface of the cork, occupying tire cavity of the female screw, being, in like manner, thickly coated with the cement in question.

The more effectually to guard against contingencies, the glass tumbler m, holding half a pint, is secured by means of the cement above mentioned, upon the plane surface of the block, exactly in the centre of the circular mercurial channel in which the bell-glass is deposited.

At a distance of somewhat more than two inches from the platina wire helix, which has been already described, and against the opposite sale of the glass vessel a second and precisely similar platina wire ascends, and passing over the edge of the tumbler,[1] where it is fastened by cement, proceeds obliquely downwards until it dips to the bottom of the circular mercurial trough, and is carried beneath the edge of the glass air-bell.

As respects the voltaic battery employed in conjunction with the apparatus I have been endeavouring to explain, I have thought it only necessary to figure the terminal cells of the arrangement, from one of which proceeds the positive polar wire until it falls into the mercurial cup o ; and from the other the consequently negative wire n, the termination of which is brought in contact, beneath mercury, with the platina wire arising from out of the glass tumbler within the air-bell to which we have frequently alluded. The polar wires are of soft copper, about one-sixteenth of an inch in thickness.

The form of constant battery, to which preference has been given on this occasion, consists of ten voltaic pairs, arranged after the following manner. The jars, composing the outer series of cells, arc of hard brown stone ware, three inches and five eighths in diameter, and five and a half inches in depth, internal measurement. In the centre of each stoneware cell is placed an excellent porous earthen tube, one quarter of an inch in thickness, the cavity of which is two inches in diameter and six in length, the bottom being formed of pipe-clay well rammed down, while in a plastic state, to about three-fourths of an inch in thickness, a method which is found to answer much better than a solid earthen baked bottom, the latter being sure to crack, even with a very moderate degree of use. Each porous tube rises about three-fourths of an inch above the top of its respective stoneware jar, a plan which greatly facilitates the convenience of manipulation.

A series of zinc and copper arcs, the pairs being united by a ribbon of the latter metal, half an inch in width, arc let full into the arranged cells, a zinc plate, two inches wide and five long, occupying the porous tube of one jar, while its corresponding copper, four inches square, and bent into a semicircular form, embraces the outside of the porous tube placed vertically within the next stoneware cell ; and so on in the usual order of combination.

As in commencing the experiment a very long-continued action was anticipated to be necessary, several series of the zinc and copper arcs, of the exact description above stated, were provided in the first instance, in order to meet the absolute necessity of changing the pairs occasionally, as the zinc plates should become reduced in size, or disappear from decomposition. The forms of the arcs employed proved exceedingly well suited to this expediency, as they were easily replaced by fresh ones, without loss of time, which might have vitiated the experiment.

When the battery was brought into operation, the stoneware cells were charged with a saturated solution of sulphate of copper, and replenished with crystals of the same salt, on occasion, as usual; and in order to avoid the formation of unnecessary saline compounds, the porous earthen tubes occupied by the zinc plates were filled with water alone.

Adjacent to the shore, and about two miles from the town of Sandwich, there exist immense ridges of silicious stones, from which the waters have long since retired. These stones have, doubtless, at some former period, been rounded by the long- continued action of the ocean into what we now provincially denominate "bowlders." One of these, weighing from four to five pounds, I selected for my purpose; and having broken it with a hammer, I obtained several pieces of fine black flint from the central part of the stone. These were made red hot in a wind furnace, then quenched in water, and reduced, in an iron mortar, to a state of very fine powder. To one ounce of this powder I added three ounces of carbonate of potass, and fused the whole into a dark green glass, by means of a furnace heat directed for a considerable time upon a Hessian crucible, in which the mixture had been previously made. Upon removing the crucible from the fire, its contents were immediately discharged into a stoneware jar, containing a pint of boiling distilled renter, which, having closely covered, I left standing for the space of six hours, when the solution was carefully filtered through Dutch paper, under cover of a large glass receiver occasionally employed in my laboratory manipulations for the purpose of screening delicate processes from the action of dust and currents of air. The operation of filtering having been completed, about half a pint of the clear solution of silicate of potass thus obtained was poured into the tumbler n, when the bell-glass which had in the mean time been made hot over a clear fire, and then carefully wiped from every particle of dust and other matter, was instantly brought over and deposited in the circular mercurial trough of the block the rim of the bell dipping at least three-tenths of an inch beneath the surface of the metal, from which, op to the date hereof, it has never been removed, or in any way encountered the slightest disturbance.

While the operation of filtering the solution was in progress, the cells of the sustaining battery were charged agreeably to the conditions formerly stated ; and now, the wire from the zinc side of the arrangement being let fall into the mercurial cup and the wire u, from the copper side brought into contact with the platina wire beneath the mercury of the circular trough, electro-chemical decomposition was observed immediately to commence in the silicate. This was exactly at seven o'clock on the evening of the 3rd of December, 1840, and, subject only to the momentary interruptions unavoidably created by the substitution of new voltaic pairs, one, two, or three at the time,as occasion might require, streams of gas have continued more or less, as influenced by temperature and other circumstances, to ascend from live platina electrodes within the glass tumbler n, through a period of more than thirteen months.

The principles of action constantly maintained by this form of apparatus, will at once be so obviously self-evident to every electrician, that I purposely refrain from observations thereon; and shall merely state that, as the slow decomposition of the silicate advanced, the gases thence arising were frequently seen to escape through the orifice of the bent tube beneath the surface of the mercury in the cup and no where else; a fact which, I presume, may be taken in proof that the bell glass and its immediate appendages had been mounted with a sufficient degree of care to exclude every other species of communication with the external atmosphere.

Recent experience having shown that electro-crystallization and other voltaic processes proceed with greater uniformity and effect when excluded from the action of light, immediately that our arrangements had been completed, means were adopted to place the entire apparatus in absolute darkness, to which it has since been constantly subject, except when thrown open for a few minutes to admit of the requisite occasional attention.

I need not trespass on the time of the Society by a long detail of unimportant circumstances incident to the entire progress of the experiment, but will submit to his notice a few extracts from original memoranda which were at first intended merely for my private information.

"1841, January 12th. — No remarkable change has yet obtained in the silicate, although it is evident that a voltaic current of considerable intensity is almost uniformly passing through the apparatus. Severe continued frost has prevailed during nearly a month; congelation, however, has been prevented in the battery cells, by the constant use of moderate fires in the apartment."

"February 2nd. — The action of the battery has recently become much more energetic, and abundant streams of gas are now continuously ascending from each platina electrode. The mercury in a Fahrenheit's thermometer, suspended in an adjoining room without fire, has been for several days past from eight to ten degrees below the freezing point. I am entirely indebted for the preservation of the voltaic process to a frequent employment of my stove, independently of which, freezing must inevitably have taken place throughout the cells of the arrangement"

"April 12th. — Decomposition is proceeding vigorously, but the platina wires are, as yet, bright and free from deposit of any kind. Found several of the zinc plates (one-sixteenth of an inch in thickness) nearly destroyed : these were replaced for the first time. The silicate has now assumed a turbid and somewhat milky character. A very remarkable appearance has taken place over a considerable extent of the inner surface of the bell-glass, and consists in certain groups or clusters of small greyish-white spots, such as would happen from accidental splashing with a wet brush, or from the operation called sprinkling by bookbinders."

" April 18th. — A great change is now evident in the solution, which, for some time past, has been gradually acquiring more and more of a milky appearance. The negative wire is completely enveloped by a moss of gelatinous silica. Streams of gas arise plentifully from both platina electrodes."

Subsequently to the date of the last extract, the turbid appearance of the solution continued greatly to increase, and tire gelatinous matter to accumulate about the negative wire beneath the surface of the fluid. Around the positive wire, and within the solution also, a dark greyish spongy aggregation took place, closely resembling in its external character the protoxide of platina. Here and there a minute crystal was formed over the copper wire m, and some few also occurred on the inner surface of the air-bell, amidst the splashes or groups of spots before- mentioned. At length, towards the end of October, tire solution in the tumbler n was reduced by electro-chemical action to about two-thirds of its original quantity, and became more like a thin milky jelly than any thing else with which I might invite comparison, except where, immediately surrounding the negative wire, a whitish silicious incrustation, several lines in thickness, had lately arisen, and to this a large flocculent mass of gelatinous silicate seemed more especially to be attracted. Continuous streams of gas were no longer seen to ascend from this electrode, but large bubbles were gradually produced, as the gaseous results of voltaic action escaped with apparent difficulty through various fissures in the silicious incrustation. From the positive wire an uniform gaseous stream arose as usual, notwithstanding the loose spongy deposit on its surface had materially increased.

My visits to the battery apparatus were now frequent, and, one day in the lost week of October, while applying a microscope very attentively to examine some appearances within the air-bell, I felt convinced that I saw an insect, having the exact character of the Acarus Crossi, the figure of which had long been perfectly familiar to me, fall slowly through the atmosphere
- Subsequent observations have induced a belief that this "spongy aggregation" is pure silicon.

of the bell, as though it had been accidentally detached from a dark cavity in the neck of the apparatus occasioned by the brass mounting. The intense degree of interest excited by this incident, I have no doubt caused on involuntary, as well as an irregular, movement of the hand, in consequence of which, the insect was suddenly lost out of the focus of my lens, and, notwithstanding my repeated efforts at that period, I could not find the creature again, and therefore refrained from any mention of the circumstance.

About the 16th of November, I observed that the silicate in the tumbler n had become much more transparent in its general appearance; and, to me, it seemed as though the greater portion of silicious matter previously held in solution, had now been attracted to the negative pole. At this time I resolved to examine the apparatus daily; and, on the afternoon of the 25th November, while engaged in using a microscope to the groups of spots or splashes as I have hitherto denominated them, and which I now found to consist in an infinitude of extremely minute pyramidal crystallizations of flinty quartz, I discovered five perfect insects, the exact representatives of those which originally appeared in the Broomfield experiments, crawling freely about on the inner surface of the bell glass: two were full grown, the rest in a less forward state.

Since the date last mentioned, insects of the character in question have been repeatedly seen within the apparatus by myself and others; sometimes in pairs; occasionally three or four (large and small) in a group; but more frequently they have appeared separately; nor have more than four ever been seen at one and the same lime since the day on which they were first discovered. In a single instance only, I observed one insect gradually disentangle itself and ascend out of the gelatinous accumulation around the negative wire beneath the surface of the fluid, and, continuing his progress, at leisure, until he got outside of the tumbler, speedily make for a dark recess afforded by the circular mercurial trough formed in the block supporting the bell-glass. Indeed, as soon as the light is let in, these creatures, in most instances, scamper away, and, apparently, without loss of time, find refuge in some cavity connected with the interior of the apparatus. However, from what I have seen, I am led to imagine that they go down at times to the silicious incrustations in the tumbler n, and — it may be — for the purpose of feeding there occasionally ; an opinion somewhat strengthened by the fact that when they are found abroad and stationary, their favourite locality seems to be amidst the groups of flinty crystals to which I have before alluded. Whether, influenced by the circumstances of their situation or otherwise, they sometimes feed upon each other, is a question I will not take upon me yet to determine, although I think appearances are certainly in favour of the con- clusion. By the aid of my microscope I have several times detected a dead insect adhering to the inner surface of the bell, and, hovering round, or in actual contact with the defunct, a vigorous individual of his species. After a few observations continued from day to day, the dead insect — gradually lessening in bulk from the first — has entirely disappeared.

For the formation of the several groups of apparently flinty quartz crystals it does not seem easy to account, unless upon the supposition that they have originated in deposits from evaporation arising from the surface of the silicate. I would by no means desire to indulge in speculations of any kind on the present occasion; yet, it is certainly a remarkable fact that these groups of crystals occur on the south side of the bell-glass and no where else; and, moreover, that several of the acari, absolutely microscopic when they were first observed, have remained attached in this situation until clearly visible to the naked eye when their free locomotion commenced.

With a view to escape confusion, I have hitherto omitted to state, that at the precise moment, when the experiment I have been detailing was undertaken, a second arrangement, in every respect similar to the first, was adopted, with the exception that the glass-bell connected therewith was charged with oxygen gas instead of atmospheric air, and a voltaic current of low tension, from a water battery of twenty pairs of zinc and copper cylinders, made to act upon the silicate. Within the air-bell of this arrangement no insects have yet been discovered; its electrochemical powers are necessarily inferior to those of the sulphate of copper battery; decomposition therefore proceeds slowly, but the solution has assumed a milky opacity and is become somewhat coagulated, and I look forward with confidence to the appearance of insects in this experiment also at no distant period.

At present I have little more to add. The experiment in which the Acarus Crossi has actually appeared, under the circumstances previously stated, still goes on, and, as various evidences indicate that a further development of insect life is in progress, it will be several months at least, ere I shall venture on its interruption. I will now merely remark, that it seems quite impossible, in the case before us, for animal life to have entered the bell-glass from without: it must in some way or other have been occasioned by the process within, but, like my predecessor, Andrew Crosse, Esq., I abstain from theorising upon the very surprising phenomena I have witnessed. I have aimed to render a simple detail of facts, and as such I submit this report to men of science, independent of commentary.

Influenced not merely by my own wishes, but much more so by the kind suggestions of others, it is my intention to continue these experiments, and to adopt even closer investigation, on this interesting and most extraordinary subject It is of the utmost consequence to science, that the strictest possible caution should be employed. I have been advised by my friend Mr. Crosse, with a most scrupulous regard for accuracy of result, to obtain the requisite quantity of mercury for my future experiments, by distillation from its sulphuret, artificially made, &c., &c.; and, in conclusion, I most cordially invite others to join me in working out this mysterious inquiry, subject to the severest restrictions which ingenuity and science can devise for the occasion.

Sandwich, January 4, 1842.

P.S. January 12th. — Winter in this part of England has set in somewhat severely during the past week. The ground has been uniformly covered with snow; Fahrenheit's thermometer without doors frequently descended to 27°; a dense veil of stratus cloud, impervious to the solar beams, seemed as it were to conspire with a bleak north-east wind in heightening the gloom and rigidity of the season. These conditions of atmosphere appear to operate unfavourably on the Acari; for, notwithstanding that my stove has again been put into requisition to obviate the effects of cold, not a single specimen has ventured out of its hiding-place for many days past, and all symptoms of forthcoming insect organization are apparently undergoing temporary suspension.

January 15th, noon.—On the morning of yesterday a genial thaw commenced, and, although the thermometer stands at this moment at 35° in the shade, with a bright blue sky, light airs from the south-west, and a general temperature considerably below that of the 14th, a very fine and full grown acarus has just ventured down the neck of the bell to the silicious incrustations mentioned in the preceding paper. One of my scientific friends who had not met with a previous opportunity of beholding these curious and extraordinary creatures, being immediately sent for, agreeably to request, having now arrived, the light from an adjacent window was permitted to fall freely upon the insect, and, as usual, operated to induce a speedy retreat to the dark chamber of its habitation.

Amidst a valuable accumulation of correspondence, rendered more estimable by numerous kind suggestions, with which I have been favoured since a partial knowledge of the experimental investigations now detailed first found its way to the public, a philosophical friend in Edinburgh, for whose literary talents the scientific and reading world generally, as well as myself, have the highest regard, writes me in reference to some brief notices which had been hastily forwarded to him, as follows; and I trust he will not be displeased with the use I am disposed to make of his very interesting communication.

" Mr. ---, an uncommonly clever young teacher of chemistry
here, and ---, says he could not have desired any thing of the

kind to be more carefully done. I may mention, however, that another able young chemist of my acquaintance has great fears as to the wood on which your experiment was conducted, baked as that was, seeing that insect ova stand so much heat, and that acari are developed so often in wood." It is, indeed a fact, that insect ova bear very great degrees of heat without having their vitality destroyed, and equally so that acari are frequently developed in ligneous substances. On a subject fraught with such an intense degree of interest as the investigation now before us seems naturally to involve, I would be among the first to remark that too much caution cannot possibly be adopted. No pains should be spared, — no difficulties, however embarrassing, permitted to check the opening of a clear path to sound and legitimate conclusion. And, although I am persuaded that insect life would have been manifested within my apparatus, even if my mercurial trough had been formed from glass or porcelain instead of wood, and in the absence of the slightest tincture of animal or vegetable matter, I feel, notwithstanding, much pleased with an opportunity to acknowledge the laudable cautiousness entertaned by the gentleman alluded to, and the more so, as his obliging remarks induce me to explain, through this note, what I have omitted to state more appropriately in the preceding paper; viz., that the platform of wood, upon which my bell glass rests, was, previously to its being worked up for use, subjected for about five hours to a degree of heat which proved adequate to its complete carbonization to the depth of full two-tenths of an inch below the surface. This fact, my young friend will probably agree with me, might be held as a

security against the after development of acari. The preparation of the wood constituting my mercurial trough, does not, however, render the suggestion, that every species of doubtful element should be kept out of the way, at all less important; and not one of the least advantages of such precaution would be the exclusion of mere cavillers from the arena of disputation. I have now the satisfaction to add, that I am at this time engaged in the construction of an arrangement for further investigations, into which nothing will be admitted except glass, platina wires passing through metallic plugs, and the solution to be acted upon by the voltaic current, unless we take into the account a small volume of mercury (distilled from its sulphuret) which, operating as a valve for the escape of gaseous matter, is placed under peculiar conditions on the outside of the generating apparatus.
Sandwich, February 24th, 1842.

Sandwich, 27th Feb. 1842.
My dear Sir,

In a paper recently committed to your kind management, relative to an experimental investigation, in which certain insects of the Acana genus appeared under very extraordinary circumstances, and incident to the operation of a voltaic current, you will find it stated, that a second arrangement, in every respect similar to the first, had been simultaneously adopted, with tire exception only, that the glass bell, forming an essential part of the apparatus, had, in the last instance, been charged with oxygen gas instead of atmospheric air, and connected with a water battery of low tension. I think you will find in my allusions to the apparatus with the oxygen bell, that I have said, "I look with confidence to the appearance of insects in this experiment also at no distant period." The sanguine anticipation has been realised. Yesterday morning, at sunrise, I visited the batteries, as is customary with me at that hour. The window of the apartment has a south-eastern aspect, and, on removing the screen ordinarily employed to exclude light, the solar beams fell with a genial influence upon the oxygen bell. Almost immediately after, on applying a lens of very moderate power, I perceived some eight or ten full-grown Acari in vigorous locomotion on the inner surface of the air-bell, and upon the outside of the tumbler containing the solution subject to the electric-current. Though I do not pretend to assign any reason why the atmosphere of this bell should be more favourable than the other to the progress of insect life, I feel no hesitation in saying that the Acari, in this experiment, appear to me decidedly larger and more vigorous than those first produced.

I will, with your permission, here avail myself of the opportunity to explain that the primary motive for having charged one of the bell-glasses allied to this investigation with pure oxygen gas, was that of providing against a very commonly urged objection,— that the ova of the insects in question might, a priori, be present in the atmosphere in which the experiment took place. Now, unless anybody will undertake to show that the germs of insect life existed in peroxide of manganese, and escaped safely out of a red-hot iron bottle along with the oxygen in its way to the glass receiver, it is clear in this experiment that they could not be present beforehand ; and, although we are acquainted with the fact that gaseous matter does actually suffer considerable changes and admixture even when confined in sound glass vessels, it has never yet been suspected that the ova of insects, however minute, could permeate a vitreous material.
I am, my dear Sir, very truly yours,
W. H. Weeks.

To Charles V. Walker, Esq.,
Hon. Sec. to the London Electrical Society.

Although the following Letter was received from Mr. Weekes after the meeting on which these reports were read, yet from the value of the information it conveys, and on account of its intimate connection with the descriptive account of the several arrangements; the Secretary deems it advisable to insert it along with Mr. Weekes' previous communication, in order that members may receive, with the least possible delay, all available information on a subject so replete with interest.

Sandwich, 19th March, 1842.

Mr Dear Sir,
Since I had the pleasure of transmitting to you a brief report of ray second voltaic experiment, incident to which the Acarus Crossi appeared within a limited atmosphere of oxygen gas, I have been favoured with several, communications from scientific individuals desirous of ascertaining the mode, by which the oxygen was procured and transferred to the bell glass, employed on the occasion. If I have not already occupied too much of the Society's attention, and an undue share of room in their valuable Transactions, in order that nothing may be left doubtful, I would gladly add the following in reply to my inquiring friends generally: —

The oxygen employed for the purpose in question was procured from peroxide of manganese, brought to an intense heat in an iron bottle; the pure gas only being conveyed into the bell-glass, through a copper tube first made quite clean. The bell-glass itself was placed for the occasion in a sand bulb, heated to about 460 degrees of Fahrenheit; the curved end of the copper pipe being carried under the rim of the receiver dipping beneath the surface of the sand, and an orifice on the top of the bell meanwhile left open, all the atmospheric air was thus driven out; and many volumes of oxygen passed through, moreover, after the purity of the gas had been ascertained. I thought this plan better than charging the bell in the first instance with water, and then displacing it by the introduction of a volume of gas, as is usual in pneumato-chemical operations.

In an experiment, accompanied by results at first thought so very mysterious, it is, perhaps, not at all surprising, that numerous suggestions should obtain relative to the probability of acari being developed from the materials used in the construction of the apparatus. Anxious to remove every trace of ambiguity connected with an inquiry of such interest, I would avail myself of the present opportunity also to communicate the exact nature of the linseed oil varnish with which the wooden platform, mentioned in my first report, is stated to have been saturated. The composition is as follows :—Drying oil, (prepared for the use of house painters, by boiling protoxide of lead in oil of linseed) six ounces; rectified oil of turpentine, and pure naphtha (commonly called rectified oil of tar,) each three ounces. The mixture arising from the thorough incorporation of these ingredients was applied while in a state of moderate ebullition, and solely with a view to preclude the absorption of moisture, atmospheric air, and other gaseous matter, by the porous structure incident to all ligneous organizations.
I am, my dear Sir, with much esteem,
Very sincerely yours,
W. H. Weekes.
To Charles V. Walker, Esq.
lion. Sec. to the Loudon Electrical Society.

www.ingramcontent.com/pod-product-compliance
Lightning Source LLC
Chambersburg PA
CBHW051717040426
42446CB00008B/927